AF248723

The Great Horned Owl's Proclamation and Other Hoots

The Great Horned Owl's Proclamation and Other Hoots

by

Louise M. Jaffe

with Owlustrations by

Jane Madson

RIVERCROSS PUBLISHING, INC.
New York · Orlando

ISBN: 0-944957-90-0

Library of Congress Catalog Card Number: 96-52908

First Printing

Library of Congress Cataloging-in-Publication Data

Jaffe, Louise M.
    The great horned owl's proclamation and other hoots / by Louise M. Jaffe ; with owlustrations by Jane Madsen.
        p.   cm.
    ISBN 0-944957-90-0 (hc)
    1. Owls--Poetry.   I. Title.
PS3560.A313G74   1997
811'.54--dc21

                                    96-52908
                                       CIP

DEDICATION

To my husband Leo Gerber, without whose constant encouragement, inspiration, creative suggestions, and late nights of typing them, these hoots would have remained unheard; my son Aaron Jaffe, without whose owlish appearance as a baby, I might never have given much of a hoot about his feathered foster-siblings; and all those generous people who have added fuel to the fire of my owl-mania by adding to my owl-hoard – these include Leo, Aaron, my dear friends Inge Auerbacher and Sophie Bravet, Ernestine and Harry Bieber, William Carlson, Annette Feldman, Jack Feldman, Harry and Lillian Felberg, Frank Giambrone, Roslyn Rabin, Ted Simon, Irwin Tuck, Alice and Norman Warwick, Nick Apongalook of the Native American Yupik and Delaware tribes, my colleagues in the Department of English at Kingsborough Community College, and Eleanor Boyle, a fellow owlcoholic and pen pal in Florida; and all the owls in the world, this book is lovingly dedicated.

CONTENTS

FORE-HOOT

To choice hoots let us welcome you
And hope you'll find them sage and true.
We've researched conscientiously
You humans from our favorite tree,

Your habits savage, habits grand,
Some even we can't understand,
But most set our suspicions bloomin'
In many ways we're rather human.

We fly with wings, you fly in planes,
But happily we both have brains
That sometimes labor overtime
Smoothing hootings into rhyme.

You eat chicken; we eat mice.
No doubt you think that's not so nice.
But much you do, when scrutinized,
Might well be tagged uncivilized.

We're known to most as birds of prey,
Sting with regrets things got that way.
Our wingèd magic's quite unique -
To convince you's what we seek

As we share our feathered flight
With hoots to startle and delight.

The Great Horned Owl's Proclamation and Other Hoots

PORTRAIT OF ONE OWLCOHOLIC
AS AN ABERRATION

An owlcoholic once did dwell.
She liked our species oh so well
She stuffed her rooms with sundry sorts
Of owls. We've even heard reports

She birthed a son, round face, large eyes.
He hooted in her fantasies
Till he grew older, keener-seeing,
Protested, "I'm a human being."

This wasn't quite enough to cure her.
Her madness was enough to lure her
To cram owl pictures, figurines
Into her house, hang sylvan scenes

With us on almost every wall.
Her friends asked, "Is she sane at all?"
When she retired from full-time work
She had more time for her bird-quirk,

Wrote owl-poems ridiculous
Pretending she was one of us.
As if that's not enough, to boot
She dubbed each one of them a hoot.

WISDOM EXERCISED

Athena was so very wise
When she chose us as her own.

She could have window-shopped the skies,
Chosen crows, left owls alone.

Yet, clever goddess, well she knew
Owls think; therefore, we hoot.

She soon concluded what she'd do -
A brilliant choice. Besides, we're cute.

Owl is what I'm often called
But just in certain places.
Say it in others and folks scowl
With very puzzled faces.

In Germany they call me *eule*
Peculiar as it seems.
In Portugal I'm a *coruja*
As I fly high in dreams.

In Latin the word for me is *bubo*,
In Ancient Greek *Athene*
After wisdom's deity -
To Arachne she was a meanie.

In Japan I'm *mimi zuku*
If I'm a barn owl.
But there *fukuru* I am called
If I'm sans ears. Seem foul?

In Dutch if my ears are long
People call me *ransuil*.
But if I was born with short ears
Then they call me *velduil*.

In France the general word for me
Is masculine: *l'hibou*.
But female owls are *chouettes*.
Which makes more sense to you?

In China I'm called *mau tau ying*,
An eagle with cat's head.
In Italy I'm called *gufo*.
I get discomforted

Not knowing what to call myself.
Identity crisis acute!
But whatever name they call me
My language is pure hoot.

THE GREAT HORNED OWL'S PROCLAMATION

I don't do mornings.
Forever it's true.
I'm strictly for nighttime.
Why aren't you?

I've never dug sunshine;
Should be no surprise.
Obnoxious sunbeams
Are bad for my eyes.

Each creature, I guess,
Has its pet time of day.
The darker the better,
I always say.

Night's the right time
For flexing my wings
When I don't get sidetracked
By day's hackneyed things.

Ask me to hoot
To greet or give warnings
But be wise enough
Not to say, "Please do mornings."

Mornings were never
The right owl-stuff.
They make my wings itchy;
They make my life rough.

I don't do mornings
And I never will.
It's no hooter's duty.
Stop asking! Be still!

AUDITORY

In darkness we can find our prey
Though others must use clues from day.

We track them down solely by sound
Though birds that can't do this abound.

In fact some of them get quite zealous
And like to mob us -- bet they're jealous! --

Heckle us rather than agree
To their inferiority.

What's more, they oversimplify
Our situations as we fly.

Our hearing should make our prey fear us
If we make sure that they don't hear us.

COMPARATIVE NUTRITION

"Yuck!" dull-sighted humans say
About the mice we love to eat.
Since this is what we hunt each day
These judges deem us indiscreet.

Who says they can cast these aspersions
About what helps keep us alive?
Do we scorn their impure diversions
Or jobs they hold from nine to five

That turn them into taut-nerve wrecks
Who seldom sleep, just toss and turn
Then can't enjoy their food or sex?
We wonder, won't they ever learn

To understand our well-earned meals
We find more irresistible
Than each poor chicken that appeals
To them, makes human stomachs full?

Who stole their minds? Why can't they see
We're no less civilized than they?
What's more, our tasty meals are free.
For most of theirs crude humans pay.

DIETARY

Tigers, tigers of the night
Is this appellation right?

We hungry owls take delight
In eating anything in sight

Yet maybe it's high time to fight
This nasty human name-call blight.

"Mr. Owl ate my metal worm."
One human wrote that loathsome palindrome.

It made many owls who heard it squirm
Because we knew a fate so wearisome

Would make our stomachs puffy and upset,
Our appetites flying quite far away.

"How down-sized can an owl's power get?"
Was all that we could find the strength to say.

How dopey does that joker think we are?
Why would we eat a metal anything?

Even a metal *mouse* would not go far
With us. An owl is no ding-a-ling!

PELLET-POEM

When you've found an owl's pellet
Do not smell it, sell it, tell it
To anyone who might dispel it.

These balls of undigested fur
And bones can stoke a mighty stir,
Most owl-mavens will concur.

Neath owl roost, in owl nest
An owl-pellet can attest
To what we owls can't digest.

They help tell what we like to eat.
Regurgitation can be sweet,
Make owl-watchers' days complete.

Next time you see one anywhere
Don't make a face! Do what is fair!
Handle it with respect and care!

ENCOUNTER

Into the woods Little Riding Hoot went,
This Pure Little Owl. She was intent

On making her way to her sick grandma's house
And bringing her a delicious mouse.

But the Great Horned Owl was swooping about.
(When he was needy, he could prove a lout.)

I'll leave you to figure what happened next.
(It's too raunchy for this pristine context!)

LOVE-HOOT

Romeo, a great horned owl,
Falls in love with human heads

Cause they're shaped the way his is,
Has fantasies of feathered beds

Where he can spend extended nights
With many human Juliets

And learn how skylike love can be.
But will he find them? Any bets?

MISUNDERSTOOD

Lucifer, the Bad Luck Owl's
Known to bode swift-winged disaster.
"Bird of evil! To the bowels
Of the earth sink faster, faster!"

Scream hysterics who can't see
Lucifer's a charming fellow
Hooting in his special tree
Watching them with eyes bright yellow.

How he got his reputation
None of us can quite recall
But he deserves its refutation.
Do it now! Don't hoot or stall!

H
O
HOOT!
HOOT!
O
HOOT!

REQUEST

Love us with your eyes
Not your raptor hands.
Anyone with wisdom
Quickly understands

Hands are used to capture.
We need to be free.
That's our special rapture,
Wingèd ecstasy.

Love us with your glances
Not your greedy touch.
Being seen entrances
Us so very much.

Give a hoot about us
In the proper way.
There's no cause to doubt us
Or what we've got to say.

Love us with your seeings.
Let your hands get rest.
We are clever beings.
We know just what's best.

It's Owl-Dad who nabs the prey
And Owl-Mom who nourishes.
Owlets know everything's O.K.
Nest-normalcy then flourishes.

Some "liberated" owl-soul,
Impatient and so glib,
Might want to know "But what's the role
Of long-due Owlettes' Lib?"

"It seems to me you shouldn't ask.
Leave owl-enough alone.
Making waves is not your task.
Go find a rodent bone

And stuff your pouting mouth with it
So you can ask no more
Upsetting questions. Quick! Admit
It's time you learned the score.

Wise owls love the status quo
And wouldn't change a thing.
So tell your questions where to go -
(We mean dust-gathering.)"

That's just how I would hoot her way
If she'd dare fly near me
Deluded that she'd have her say
For she-owl liberty.

I wouldn't give the slightest hoot
If she should hear, then scowl
And think she's so stylishly cute.
So call me Male Chauvinist Owl.

OWL MODESTY

Our feathers never let us be
Naked so immodestly
As humans are when bathing and
Others things, you understand,

Just mentioning would make us blush
So they'll remain a tactful hush.
At least we claim a hoot-felt shame.
Though known as raptors, far from tame,

We've learned what it's not right to bare.
It isn't right; it can't be fair
To copy humans, who undress,
Stand brazen in their nakedness.

Surely they could use feathers, too,
Memos of what they shouldn't do.

Most of us are monogamous
Because quite wisely we've decided
To eschew all that messy fuss
That ensues when hoots get divided

Among too many a feathered mate.
On whose frequency would we hoot
For instance, then? We'd vacillate,
Splice indecisiveness to boot.

Moreover we avoid diseases
With avian fidelity.
Knowing who's whose always pleases
Because it leaves us sweetly free

To swoop and soar beneath the stars,
Plop pellets down as souvenirs
Sans polygamy's nasty scars
And STD-related fears.

THE ENCYCLOPEDIA SAYS...

Disks of radiating feathers
Frame our forward-facing eyes,
Helping folks through varied weathers
Get convinced that we are wise.

What is more and what is good
Owls sport a range of sizes.
Not so quickly understood,
We are full of huge surprises.

Just six inches, humans say,
Are saw-whet, pygmy, and elf,
Two feet, eagle, hawk, horned, gray.
An owl would mistake itself

For something else were we not blessed
With wisdom so spectacular,
Home-grown in every owl-nest
As owlets learn just who they are.

Owl-feathers make no noise.
It's hard to hear when we're around.

One of countless owl-joys,
Clever feathers free of sound.

Who said owl-feathers should be
Empty-head dead giveaways?

With muted feathers we fly free
In wide-eyed unexpected ways.

<pre>
          HOOT!
            O
     H   O
     HOOT!
       O
HOOT!
</pre>

LAMENT OF THE SPOTTED OWLS

With cruelty too tightly linked
Of humans, we might be extinct.
"Let's hoard our timber!" is their cry.
They don't care if we live or die.

We've been around for centuries,
Proudly perched in our pet trees.
Now who are they to say time's come
For us to be hootless, a/k/a/ dumb?

We don't think it's our time to go.
We've got too much to live and know,
Too many tasty mice to eat
Before we deem our lives complete.

Why are these humans playing God?
They're not very P.C. or mod.
But we know they don't see so clearly
For if they did they'd love us dearly.

We help them keep their forests clean,
Eat mice and rabbits. They're so mean
To think they'd like to wipe us out.
We know beyond the thinnest doubt

They'll miss us once we are no more.
Their lack of foresight they'll deplore
But only when it's much too late.
Why don't they stop and meditate

On evils of their greedy ways,
Misjudgments from their foolish days?
Don't they know when our homes are gone
We have no way for hooting on?

Destructive cutters should think twice,
Take time to ponder our advice
Before they do what they'll regret
In sad, hoot-muted retrospect.

MALADY

Owls in the belfry
Owls on the stairs.

Chronic owlcoholics
Hear hooting in their prayers.

Owls in their windows
Owls at their doors.

Some are owlcoholics.
What hang up is yours?

MEMO

We owls are color-blind,
A fact that might appall.

But please bear this in mind:
No one can win 'em all.

In a host of other ways
Our eyes are most outstanding,

Certainly worth your greatest praise.
Humans are too demanding!

NOCTURNAL SOVEREIGNTY

We are masters of the night
And darkness. They belong to us.
Don't dare tell us that we're not right
Or we will hoot a gruesome fuss.

We haunt dim woods better than spooks
Since midnight is our special time.
Diurnal birds might deem us kooks -
Stupid as calling hoots a crime!

High-flown kings with sylvan thrones,
We map our course by our own rules,
Guard castle-nests with high-pitched tones,
That are not taught in humans' schools.

PARADOX

Across political frontiers
We owls move freely hoot-tuned nights.
Yet very often, it appears,
We struggle about hunting rights.

We lock sharp talons, never yield
On territoriality.
Our motions seldom are concealed
Neath pretend-cordiality.

If, reader dear, it seems to you
This is hypocrisy or guile,
Think what your nation's leaders do
For crediting with feats worthwhile.

RECIPROCITY

Don't dismiss with "for the birds"
Precious owl wisdom-words

Lest we might have to teach our wings
To fly us far from human things.

When we aim our hoots at you,
Concentrate. They're clear and true.

"For the humans," we don't say
When we can't see things your way.

"For the birds" perhaps applies
To some of your philosophies

When your thoughts are circular
Since you're not smart as owls are.

HOOT-
RULES
1.
2.
3.

REMEDIATION

Though hard to believe
Or a bit convoluted,
An owlet once needed
Help when he hooted.

For frustrating days
(Don't dare mumble "a dumb thing"!)
When he did, we'd all ask
"Did he really say something?"

After resisting,
This deficient hooter
Hired a gray owl
To be his tutor.

They practiced until
Instead of cruel laughter
He heard praise, hooted
Happily long ever after.

ROLE

I'm playing Devil's Ad-voc-owl.
I'd deem it destiny most foul

To pose as Devil's Ad-vo-cat.
I'm bird, not feline. That is that.

I hoot (not mew) when I give flack,
Claim black is white or white is black.

It's dully gray when one agrees
Too often. Glib hypocrisies,

It seems to me, are born that way.
Be discreet: disagree today.

"Give a hoot. Don't pollute" -
Many humans find that cute.

But we label ludicrous
Slogans that make fun of us.

Why are humans so direct?
Can't they be more circumspect,

Recalling in their verbal dealings
As *they're* supposed to, *we* have feelings?

When we find we're trivialized
Or, uglier, vulgarized,

Our queasy egos shrink to dust
And we find humans hard to trust.

We wish they'd take the time to see
We, too, need our dignity.

SPECIES CROSS

Ever note the newest humans
Have faces very much like owls'
When they do their fast-paced bloomin's
With their eyes stretched wide? No scowls

From you, you proud human maker
Or your latest moon-faced chick.
Be soothed by truth. Don't be a faker
Or hide behind transparent <u>shtick</u>.

It's feathers away from putting down
To claim your baby's like a nestling.
So smile at what we hoot. Why frown?
Even brief owlhood's the best thing!

VERITIES

This timely truth
Needs to be told:
Whenever owls
Get too old

To hoot, to hunt,
To fend off tension,
Nature should offer
Us a pension.

Be prudent, then.
Reserve, provide
So all of us
Feel gratified

When humans wouldn't
Dare dispute
Our worth when we're
Too weak to hoot

Or even seem
Prone to conspire
Against us when
We owls retire.

TAKING TURNS

When our feathered heads rotate
    Clueless humans don't quite know

        Just what that might indicate -
      Do we come or do we go?

            Just because each splendid head
              Can turn one-eighty quick degrees,

           Some humans get discomfited
            Or think we owls are oddities.

            It's about time humans learned
          When another living thing

        Has a head more widely turned
       It is not an underling.

      Half-circle both ways our heads spin
    As readily as we gulp mice.

    And now it's time that we begin
  To hoot you overdue advice:

Never mock our heads' rotations
Unless you want ignorance showing.

You might feel smug in your condemnations
But at least *we* know if we're coming or going.

AFTER-HOOT

Now that you have listened well
To all our hoots were meant to tell

We hope that you will leave here changed,
Your thinking somewhat rearranged,

At least where owls are concerned.
We've tried to make sure you have learned

We hooters merit your respect.
You have no reason to object.

We're friends of night. Stars know we're wise.
We're blessed with elephantine eyes.

Athena made no silly fuss.
Instantly she adopted us.

All know she was a clever dame.
Why don't you choose to do the same?

Professor Emerita of English at Kingsborough Community College of the City University of New York, Louise Jaffe teaches creative writing as well as the more traditional literature and composition courses. She holds a B.A. from Queens College, an M.A. from Hunter College, an M.F.A. from Brooklyn College, and a Ph.D. from the University of Nebraska, and is a member of Phi Beta Kappa.

Listed in *A Directory of American Poets and Fiction Writers*, this happily incurable poetry addict has published three poetry chapbooks, had poems included in a wide variety of anthologies and literary magazines, presented warmly received poetry readings throughout New York City and environs, and won prizes in many poetry contests.